WE'RE JUST VISITING

Written By:

Titanya Johnson

Dedication

This book is dedicated to my Mother who brought me into this world and always told me I had a light to shine and i can be and do anything I want. Thank you for your words I am exactly what I want to be and more I love you continue to let your light shine Bernice King you birthed a true star However you are my 1st gift from GOD.

This book is dedicated to my 4 amazing children Epiphany, Jaymes, James and Jayson thank you for making life worth writing about you all bring out the best in me continue to let your light shine - Lastly - theres a bundle of Joy my first grandbaby I dedicate this book to you Superstar Shine the Brightest you come from Greatness! oh wait this book is dedicated to you yes you reading it .

I wrote this book with you and your family in mind so look at that you got your first Book dedication SHINE your LIGHT!

Piff . SAYS- LOOK LOOK WHAT IS THAT?

Jayson . THAT'S A SHOOTING STAR,

it's like a light in the dark sky.

Piff . Where is it going?

Jayson . its coming here on earth to bring light.

BEEP BEEP

Jayson . oh thats my Mom I gotta go.

Piff . where are you going?

Jayson . in the house to see my newborn baby brother. My mom says he is carrying great purpose, we all have great purpose on this earth.

Piff . Great purpose? What do you mean?

Jayson . Yes like that shooting star shining bright in the darkness. We are carrying a light -the light of GOD on the inside of us.

BEEP!

Piff . so your baby brother has a light in him?
Jayson . yes and so do you! And so do I, we all have a light
"We are the salt and light of the earth"
Piff . what I'm SALT? My Nana says don't use too much salt?
Wait... Where is my light? Do i need batteries?

Jayson . Haha thats a good question as for salt and light goes it's a saying out of this book my Mom reads everyday the Bible (Matthew 5:13-16)
The saying means we are on earth to add flavor and to shine so in other words
We are just passing threw We are just visiting.

Continue Jayson

`WE ARE JUST VISITING EARTH"

To carry this light.

Our light is a gift and so is our flavor we bring

(Us being our unique self). It all adds to the earth

Joy and Hope see light shines in the dark

Light helps us see

Light is like love

So while we are here like that star

we are to shine

We won't be here forever

Piff . Why not?

Jayson . Cause we have a job to LET OUR LIGHT shine then return

after we are finished our assignment. After all, We are just visiting

The earth isn't permanent

Our Bodies are not permanent

We are just visiting

Jayson . it's like going to the store for ice cream
you don't stay at the store all day
You don't live at the store forever.
You go to the store and get the ice cream and return home

Piff . Really

Jayson . yes!, really just know we
are not here forever,
And when our time to return has
come "we were just visiting"
We have a place to call home and its
outta of this world
Repeat after me were just visiting
and when its time to return home
everything is gonna be alright.
We are here to carry the light so shine
while your here visiting.

The End

www.ingramcontent.com/pod-product-compliance
Lightning Source LLC
Chambersburg PA
CBHW040253100426
42811CB00011B/1249